THE MOUNTAIN SPIRIT AND THE MOON

Written by
Haiying Wu

Translation by
Charles Nichols

Illustrated by
Chengqian Dai

SEAFLAME
Children's Books

A young mountain spirit carried a large pile of rocks around the mountain, knocking over trees left and right.

He stood at the mountain's highest peak, took a big breath in through his nose, and blew a gust of wind from the top of the mountain all the way down to the bottom.

The moon broke, one large piece falling into the lake and a small piece falling into the valley. He had roared the moon to pieces!

A broken moon hung in the sky, leaking out all its moonlight!

Wolf Cub was very worried. He could only howl under the moonlight. The tip of his nose had to point at the full moon to give him confidence.
The night grew darker and darker...
The Moon Hare couldn't find its way home.
The Sky Dog lost his drawings.

The three-legged Golden Toads saw that a piece of the moon was missing in the sky, and found it in the lake. Together, they croaked: "Oh no, oh no, the moon has fallen into the water!"

"Doesn't he know how important the moon is?" The Sky Dog asked.

"Who will go deal with him?" Wolf Cub added.

"I..."

"Why does he hate the moon?" Asked the Moon Hare.

They thought the Spider Queen was about to volunteer, but instead she said, "I found this piece of the moon in the valley."

If they could scoop the other piece of the moon out of the lake, they would be able to put the two broken pieces back together. But, how would they get it back in the sky?

They decided to drag the pieces up to the highest peak of the mountain, then discuss what to do next, even though the mountain spirit was there too. The young mountain spirit had already seen them coming from far away, and rushed down the mountain. "I'm the one who broke the moon."

Everybody stared at the spirit in shock, "You broke the moon? What were you thinking?"

"I wanted to make a giant pile of rocks so I could touch the moon. The rocks kept rolling away and wouldn't stay put."

The mountain spirit didn't realize that his shout of anger would break the moon.

"I will fix the moon if you let me touch it." But the mountain spirit didn't know how to fix the moon either. Blow the pieces back into the sky? He blew so hard flames came out of his nose, but the pieces of the moon didn't even move. Kick it up? That would only break the moon into even more pieces.

It would be best to throw it up. The mountain spirit grabbed the pieces of the moon, still wrapped in the spider's web, and flung them as hard as he could. The moon pieces fluttered through the sky and were sucked up by the moonlight, with the Spider Queen still on it!

The Spider Queen stuck the broken moon back together, and spun out a long, long ladder all the way back to the ground. "Whoever wants to touch the moon in the future, can climb up this ladder. Please don't ever break the moon again!"

The Mountain spirit and the Moon

Text copyright © 2021 by Haiying Wu
Illustrations copyright © 2021 by Chengqian Dai
All rights reserved, including the right of reproduction in whole or in part in any form.

English Translation by Charles Nichols
English edition edited by Haibo Xu

Chinese edition published under the title 小山神想干什么 by China Light Industry Press Ltd in 2022.

English translation edition published by Seaflame Children's Books with the express permission of China Light Industry Press Ltd.

The text for this book was set in Quicksand and Source Han Serif.
The illustrations for this book were created using paper cuts and pencil drawing.

Identifies:
ISBN 978-1-7782214-0-8 (eBook)
ISBN 978-1-7782214-1-5 (Paperback)
ISBN 978-1-7782214-2-2 (Hardcover)

Haiying Wu is an award-winning author of several popular children's books. Her picture book series *Wow! The Classic of Mountains and Seas* was selected for the 2020 Motion Force China Original Animation Publishing Support Program, and her book *Grandpa Likes to Hide and Seek* won the 2017 Hsin Yi Picture Book Award. She lives in Tangshan, China and Toronto, Canada.

Charles Nichols was born in Houston, Texas in 2004 and has lived in Calgary, Alberta since 2012. He has been offered admission to the University of Toronto Faculty of Arts & Science. He has long had an interest in creative writing, aspiring to have a career as a novelist.

Chengqian Dai is a young woman who paints and draws in her remote home. A gardener who dwells on her rooftop terrace. A mother who keeps busy looking after her adorable twins. A monster illustrator whose dreams transport her from reality into a world of fantastic creatures. She began to draw illustrations for magazines and books in 2003, and in 2016 she started creating picture books. She has two publications: *Yue Shen Prince Changqin* and *The Mountain spirit and the Moon* in China.

www.ingramcontent.com/pod-product-compliance
Lightning Source LLC
Chambersburg PA
CBHW041704160426
43209CB00017B/1740